Hi world,

What's going on?

Hi world,

Why the earth is dying?

Hi world,

How are the animals becoming extinct?

Hi world,

Why are there wars?

Hi world,

Who are the sinners?

Hi world,

Why people are dying?

Hi world,

Which crimes are worst toward color or non-color people?

Hi world,

Who is the solution of the problems?

Hi world,

Where is your God?

Hi world,

Why we going backwards instead of forward?

Hi world,

Are my children safe?

Hi world,

So many questions to our problems and I know they will never be fix by your seven deadly sins.

Lesson 2: Truth

The truth will always set you free when you a least

expected in your life.

The truth will always be there when you ready to face

it.

The truth will always let you know from right to wrong.

The truth will always be endangerment to you and

others.

The truth will always push you to the right path of life.

The truth will always receive light and beat the

darkness.

The truth will always be the guidance and protection.

The truth will always be a misunderstanding.

The truth will always beat the lies of deception.

The truth will always lift you up and motivate you.

The truth will always give you something to lean on.

The truth will always never let you down.

The truth will always be your best friend.

Lesson 3: Treasure

What is a treasure?

Piece of gold.

What is treasure?

Million dollars.

What is a treasure?

Diamond ring.

What is a treasure?

Range rover.

What is a treasure?

Beach house.

What is a treasure?

Vacation.

What is a treasure?

Mansion.

What is a treasure?

One hundred acres.

What is a treasure?

Beautiful children.

What is a treasure?

Spouse.

What is a treasure?

Good health.

What is a treasure?

House.

What is a treasure?

Car.

What is a treasure?

Job.

What is a treasure?

Family.

What is a treasure?

Friends.

What is a treasure?

Treasure is everything part of life but never

materialistic.

Lesson 4: To my mother, To my father

To my mother,

To the woman I look up to,

To the woman I want to be,

To the woman that never let herself down,

To the woman is beautiful like the speed of light.

To my mother,

To the woman that conquers all,

To the woman that has wisdom,

To the woman that is the leader of all women,

To the woman that love her ladybugs.

I love you with all my heart,

I know I have the best mother in the world.

To my father,

To the man that leads his family,

＼

To the man that holds so much power,

To the man never give up,

To man that has unconditional love.

To my father,

To the man that sees the future,

To the man that is an aura of full of light,

To the man that has strong will,

To the man that follows the truth.

I love you with all my heart,

I know I have the best father in the world.

Lesson 5: Lover

To my lover,

Have you always loved me for me.

To my lover,

Have you always fought for me.

To my lover,

Have you always encouraged me.

To my lover,

Have you always supported me.

To my lover,

Have you always stuck with me.

To my lover,

Have you always been my motivation.

To my lover,

Have you always criticized me.

To my lover,

Have you always been my down fall.

To my lover,

Have you truly understood me.

To my lover,

Have you always been the one for me.

Lesson 6: Look at Me

Past: Hey Rica!

Present: Hello!

Past: Look at me! What do you see?

Present: I see a little girl that evolve into a beautiful woman.

Past: Look at me! What do you hear?

Present: I hear the little girl world pool that will stay through her adulthood.

Past: Look at me! What do you smell?

Present: I smell the little girl fear throughout her body that drench her youth to elderly.

Past: Look at me! What do you taste?

Present: I taste the little girl freedom and success that will reflect throughout her life.

Past: Look at me! What do you feel?

Present: I feel the little girl spiritual bond that gather people with her light.

Past: Look at me! What do you kick?

Present: I kick the little girl troubles away so it won't affect her future.

Past: Look at me! What do you hit?

Present: I hit the little girl people that going try to stop her way.

Past: Look at me! What do you speak?

Present: I speak to the little girl that stand up for herself in the world.

Past: Look at me! Are you satisfied?

Present: I satisfy the little girl accomplishments and where she is going on her journey.

Past: Look at me! What you do if you meet her?

Present: I meet the little girl, I would give her a hug and tell her "Its okay you made it and don't look down upon yourself".

Life

I see birds flying to the south.

Life

I see butterflies pass me by.

Life

I see squirrels climbing the trees.

Life

I see the flowers blooming.

Life

I see the kids running.

Life

I see the sun glowing.

Life

I see the bees buzzing.

Life

I see the cars passing me by.

Life

I see the music notes playing.

Life

I see the elderly resting.

Life

I see the wedding bells.

Life

I see babies being born.

Life

I see the world booming.

Life

Life is so precious and don't let it pass you by.

Lesson 8: I See You

I see you

When I look at your eyes, I see me in you

I see you

When I wipe your tears, I see my pain in you

I see you

When I feel your passion, I see my dedication in you

I see you

When I hear your heart, I see my love in you

I see you

When I see your strength, I see my strong will in you

I see you

When I absorb your light, I see my spirit in you

I see you

When I touch your happiness, I see my peace in you

I see you

When I sense your present, I see my gifts in you

I see you

When I visualize your beauty, I see my position in you

I see you

When I hug your dreams, I see my future in you

I see you

When I see through you, the world doesn't matter

Lesson 9: Brown community

Hello brown community,

I been betrayed by birth.

Hey brown community,

I been bully through my youth.

Hola brown community,

I never been accepted.

Bonjour brown community,

I been seen as an animal.

Greetings brown community,

I been abuse in every aspect.

Hi brown community,

I been lock up for life.

Ciao brown community,

I been hated and thrown away.

Hallo brown community,

I always been target.

Howzit brown community,

I always cried that my color isn't good enough for you.

As of right now, I don't need you but you need me.

Lesson 10:My people

My people

What are we doing?

My people

We are so divided

My people

We are always fighting

My people

We can't communicate

My people

We can't help each other

My people

We can't create our future

My people

What can we do?

My people

We can unite as one

My people

We can stand up for each other

My people

We can communicate and get along

My people

We can fight and protect for our future

My people

Our unity and growth are our power and key.

Without these two, we are nothing.

Bonus Song : I Don't Want to Be Here

I don't want to be here no more

I don't want to be here uh huh uh huh uh huh

I don't want to be here

I don't want to be here no more

I don't want to be here uh huh uh huh uh huh

Yea

She doesn't want to be here

She feels the world is chewing her out

Yea

She doesn't want to be here

She doesn't have no more fight in her

Let's Go

She doesn't want to be here

She feels the world is against her and she feels alone

She doesn't want to be here

Come on Girl Let's Go You got me

I don't want to be here

I don't want to be here no more

I don't want to be here uh huh uh huh uh huh

Yea

She doesn't want to be here

You don't let yourself down and pick yourself back up

She doesn't want to be here

The world is in your hands and take it Let's Go

She doesn't want to be here

You got girls by yourself and by your side

She doesn't want to be here

The ancestors got you and they won't let you go

I don't want to be here

I don't want to be here no more

I don't want to be here uh huh uh huh uh huh

Yea

She doesn't want to be here

She tired of everything Come on Girl

Everything in front your eyes

Take it and Let's Run

Ok

I don't want to be here

Yea

I don't want to be here no more

I don't want to be here uh huh uh huh uh huh

Yea

That's a wrap

Short Biography

My name is Sharika KKkyha. I was born and raised in

the state of Georgia. I have lived in Duluth for 19 years

and now I live in Lilburn. I graduated Norcross High

School. I did study psychology for 8 years and

education for 4 years. I didn't earn a degree because of

life circumstances. I took courses 2 years ago for

Special Education Advocate and I am certified in this

area. Now I am starting my journey as an author. I love

writing and expressing myself on paper. It took me 11

years to find this passion and I am motivational speaker

as well. I learned that everyone isn't meant for college

but there is career out there for someone and they just

have to look for it.

What the book is about?

The book represents the life of lessons. Every lesson I

learned through my journey of life. Some of the poems

have questions that make me think about life and the

world we are living in. The other poems just express my

emotions about what is currently going on right now. I

decided to write this book because I love writing and I

can express myself better in poems. I believe a normal

biography is boring and it isn't interesting in my

perspective. So I hope you enjoy this book and this

volume 1. More Coming Out Soon!

Made in the USA
Columbia, SC
06 March 2025

54712852R00029